Organization for Management

Donald N. Lombardi

Table of Contents

 **Introduction**

Linking People to Profit

Successful management makes successful organizations. The intelligent management of people and profit has become the critical role of business today. The planning, organizing, and controlling of management work is vital to meeting business objectives. **As the owner and/or manager of a business you are probably aware of areas in which you could operate more profitably and more efficiently**. But when you have a business to run, it is hard enough to cope with today, let alone plan for tomorrow-and have fun doing it.

We are here to help you "separate the forest from the trees". For the past twenty years we have worked with thousands of small business owners and have developed the most essential business operating procedures for success of their enterprises. **These procedures have been field tested and proven to be effective in most of our consulting assignments.**

You can use these operating procedures in multiple departments of your company immediately, and easily edit and customize them in Microsoft Word to fit your company needs.

Many organizations of all industry types and sizes have discovered the remarkable differences these operating procedures can make in achieving the following:

- A more disciplined approach to profit and growth.
- A more realistic balance between long and short term objectives.
- A better capacity for dealing with change.
- A better utilization of organizational resources; human, material and financial.
- A stronger management team.
- A more meaningful performance and control system.

Owner/Operators can save countless hours of research, planning, and development time by using prewritten policies and procedures for accounting, people management and more.

We have personally field tested and proven these operating policies and procedures to be successful in most client situations. They are now documented here and made part of three (3) different manuals: **Business Operating Procedures Manual; Profit and Expense Control Manual; and Organization for Management Manual.**

 **Managing People**

1.0 THERE IS NO "MAGIC" IN MANAGING PEOPLE!

1.1 If you want to be more effective with people you must understand that substantial increases in effectiveness have substantial costs and risks. Those cost and risks are both subtle and ego threatening; but if you are willing to accept them, there is virtually no limit to your potential for human influence. If you are not willing to accept them, then you must be content with your present level of influence, because it will not increase.

2.0 VALUES ARE THE KEY

2.1 People do not engage in behavior because it will be good for the organization or because it will serve your values. They engage in a behavior only if that it is the best behavior for them to engage in to take care of what is important to them. Your challenge in influencing others is to show how what they perceive best serves their values. These values include: self esteem, acceptance, affiliation, friendship, security, freedom, autonomy, recognition, success, and fun.

3.0 POWER

3.1 Power is the ability to affect the allocation of resources.

3.2 Authority is an organizationally granted privilege to engage in certain behaviors and expect to be supported in those activities; e.g., to hire, fire make policy and direct procedures.

3.3 Power is not authority; authority is not power.

3.4 If we want to influence others we must spend more time thinking through our words and gestures, out timing, and our approach. To do so might seem unnatural and forced.

3.5 Behaviors that feel natural are merely behaviors we have repeated many times.

3.6 What seems reasonable may be reasonable only to us. If we want to influence others we must take the time to find out what best serves their values and what is reasonable to them.

 **Managing People**

4.0   RATIONALIZATION – The First Obstacle to Effectiveness

4.1   We have learned how to find reasons for failure and lie to ourselves by blaming others. In doing so we have reduced our effectiveness.

4.2   Time spent in rationalizing is time not spent influencing others.

4.3   Rationalization is warm and comfortable.

4.4   Our lack of substantial effectiveness in influencing people is less a function of our failed attempts that it is a function of our failure to try or persist.

4.5   To try to influence or to persist in the face of rejection is to risk failure.

4.6   To rationalize is to enjoy the comfort, ease, security, and support of a well know place.

5.0   INSTALLING A NEW PROGRAM

5.1   **"Never expect anyone to engage in a behavior that serves your values unless you give that person adequate reason to do so!**

5.2   <u>It is installed by repetition.</u>

6.0   PERCEPTION – The Place Influence Resides

6.1   People have multiple values, many unrelated to money, and as long as they see that those values will be served in an acceptable way in exchange for the behavior you want, you can get anyone to do anything you want.

6.2   What you want someone to do is irrelevant to his or her decision. What is critical is that person's perception of the relationship between what you want that person to do and that person's values.

6.3   This is the necessary connection within that person's head. This is the personal, subjective, fragile, and malleable state that controls behavior.

 **Managing People**

7.0 IMPLEMENTATION – It Is All In How You Do It

7.1 **"One hundred percent of the effectiveness of any idea is the function of its implementation".**

7.2 The implementation of any idea determines how it will be perceived, and how it is perceived by those who must cooperate with it determines its effectiveness.

7.3 It is not the idea that determines success – it is the implementation of the idea!

8.0 THE COSTS OF EFFECTIVENESS

8.1 Most of the effective techniques for human influence require you to make the first move and accept vulnerability to failure.

8.2 Effectiveness requires persistence through rejections and repeated failures.

8.3 To acquire such persistence we must overcome well-worn beliefs about failure and well worn, emotional programs that have played thousands of times in our heads.

8.4 You must give up rationalizing, subject yourself to changes of unfairness, take on costly and risky behaviors, give up some long standing, feel good behaviors, and overcome your deeply entrenched fear of failure in order to increase your effectiveness in managing people.

8.5 This is neither easy nor pleasant, but no other route is powerful.

8.6 NO other route may be possible.

 **Managing People**

9.0 THE VALUES MODEL

9.1 People who you are trying to influence process the data of your attempt to influence them in terms of their:

> 9.1.1 Capability
> > Competence (knowledge and skill)
> > Confidence (can I do it?)
> 9.1.2 Perception of Value
> 9.1.3 Perception of Probability of Value
> 9.1.4 Perception of Cost
> 9.1.5 Perception of Risk

10.0 THE C.A.R.E.S. MODEL

10.1 The C.A.R.E.S. Model below shows how Management Behavior (hot buttons) motivates employees (needs satisfaction) to provide managers and customers with what they want. This model was created by me in 1972, using "Maslow's hierarchy of Needs", and has been tested and proven successful in most of my client situations.

Managing People

C.A.R.E.S.

Manager Wants	Management Behavior	Employee Needs	Customer Wants
Profit ←	Communicate →	Actualization →	Value
Production —	Appreciate —	Self Esteem →	Delivery
Loyalty ←	Respect —	Social →	Service
Efficiency ←	Educate —	Security →	Quality
Work ←	Spend —	Basic —	Product

Mission Statement

1.0 PURPOSE

1.1 A mission statement is the foundation from which the company establishes policies and procedures. This operating procedure offers a method of formulating a simplified mission statement to be used as a basis for Strategic Planning and as a communication medium for all who do business here.

2.0 CONCEPT

2.1 A mission statement communicates to employees, vendors, customers, and competitors what top management's overall expectations, direction and focus are. Goals, policies and procedures are developed within the confines set forth in the mission statement. The basic function of a mission statement is to convey to the public and employees why the company exists.

2.2 The Strategic Plan begins with the mission statement. Long range objectives are formulated from this statement. Short and long-term goals are then developed for each department, product, and function. Project Schedules are the timetables added to the goals to perpetuate and measure the progress throughout the company.

2.3 The mission statement is a written description of the ownership's vision and direction in terms easily understood by all employees. The vision is the personal way the company plans to do business. Management and employee decisions are guided by, but do not violate the mission statement. The mission statement provides a company-wide bond and a single-minded direction and focus.

3.0 MISSION STATEMENT FORMAT

3.1 The mission statement is a short message describing the company relationship and expectations with respect to customers, employees, community, and vendors. It should describe the commitment to quality, the relative price range, and the market and products the company will focus on. Use action verbs in the sentence structure.

3.2 List critical attributes necessary to instill the desired culture in the employees. Keywords are used and defined such as quality, customer service, and teamwork. The purpose is to set a common direction for everyone within the company.

Mission Statement

3.3 List what the company will provide for its employees, for its customers, for its vendors, and for the community. Develop a realistic and truthful statement of what will be provided for each of these entities.

3.4 The development of the mission statement begins with the completion of the attached form. Prioritize the list of topics as:

A-Important must be in the statement.

B-Some importance, could be in the statement.

C-Not very important, not necessary for the statement.

Next, explain what the topic means to you (your vision)

3.5 Upon completion of the form, draft the mission statement using the "A" priorities and space permitting, some of the "B" priorities. The entire mission statement may be six sentences or six short paragraphs, but must be easily understood and brief. If employees do not understand what it means, they will not respond as intended. If the mission statement is too long, the employees will not remember it.

4.0 CONCLUSION

4.1 Review the mission statement annually with employees, serving as a constant reminder as to the purpose of the company's existence. The vision for the company rarely changes. However, since the mission statement is the foundation from which the strategic plans take root, the statement must be structurally sound.

4.2 The mission statement is posted on large placards or in frames in conspicuous places as a reference for employees and managers. It is placed on all advertisements to show customers and vendors that there is a framework for decision making and performance expectations.

4.3 The Ownership is the "keeper of the vision" and the designer of the mission statement. Other management may be involved in the statement formulation but the responsibility of the completed mission statement belongs to the Ownership. The President is responsible for maintaining adherence and awareness of the mission statement throughout the company.

Mission Statement

TOPIC	IMPORTANCE	VISION – HOW DO YOU SEE THE COMPANY?
Profit	_____	_____
Market Type	_____	_____
Sales Growth	_____	_____
Company Growth	_____	_____
Customer Service	_____	_____
Competition	_____	_____
Product	_____	_____
Employees	_____	_____
Community	_____	_____
Vendors	_____	_____
Safety	_____	_____
Ethics	_____	_____

Strategic Team Operating Plan

1.0 INTRODUCTION

1.1 A roadmap is required to define and focus on an overall direction, goals, and targets that are desired by the Owner.

1.2 The strategic plan defines the foundation and the growth plans for the diversity desired by the Owner. It should include a Vision or Mission statement as well as budget pro-formas.

1.3 It will not be a rigid plan that restricts the company to a single-minded course of action, but will be an aggressive charter that specifies where the company might go and how it might get there.

1.4 The plan should not only ignite purpose and direction in the organization, but should also provide for intelligent exploration of other courses of action and changes where warranted.

1.5 If the company is to operate in the 21st Century as a professional diversified well positioned business, a Strategic Plan must be produced as a path to follow and as a measurement of the company's success toward achieving it goals.

2.0 PREPARATION OF THE PLAN

2.1 It is important for all employees (the team) to be made part of the plan and to claim ownership through participating in its development.

2.2 All employees should be interviewed by a professional outsider either in person or by use of a questionnaire and be allowed to freely express how they feel about their job, their supervision, and the company. **These conversations should be confidential**.

2.3 Management should then meet off site in a comfortable environment preferable away from the company premises.

2.4 The meeting room should be set up in a semi-circle facing a flip chart. The participants should be told that they are to THINK, LISTEN, and ASK QUESTIONS.

2.5 The Planning Session usually runs two (2) days. On day 1 the President will lead the group in visiting the company mission statement to ensure it is current. He or she will also set Goals and Objectives for the year.

Strategic Team Operating Plan

2.6 Following these discussion, the Professional who conducted the interviews and/or surveys, will now play the role of "meeting facilitator". He or she will list all of the problems and opportunities on the flip chart and explain each item so that everyone has a clear understanding. Again this is done without disclosing the source of any particular problem or opportunity expressed. As each flip chart is filled it is removed from the stand and tape on the wall so that everyone can see.

2.7 It is **IMPORTANT** for management to understand that employee expressions may only be perceptions. However, perceptions, although not real, can still be an obstacle in having everyone working together on the same team towards a common goal. Therefore, perceptions must still be dealt with in a calm and intelligent manner with facts, so that obstacles can be removed and full team effort can be gained.

2.8 On day 2, the facilitator will lead the group in discussing each of the problems and opportunities.

2.9 As each problem or opportunity is discussed an action plan must be generated and assignments made to correct the problem or develop the opportunity.

2.10 Once the plan is formulated a group meeting should be held with all employees to announce the plan.

2.11 The plan should be monitored at each management meeting as due dates are being approached to ensure that the person assigned has all the resources available to meet his due date. (It should not be viewed as an "I gotcha").

2.12 Feedback on the progress of the plan should be reported to employees at their scheduled group meetings as well.

2.13 As major milestones are achieved they should be recognized and celebrated by the full team.

 # Organization Structure

1.0 INTRODUCTION

1.1 The purpose of this procedure is to lay out the logic and methodology of the functional requirement of the company.

1.2 The procedure is presented in such a manner that the Functional Organizational Structure, the related functions, and a resulting Position Organization Chart can be developed.

1.3 This is the beginning of the process. It provides a basis of identifying the functions within the organization.

1.4 One person may perform more than one of these functions and may wear several hats within the organization. This procedure identifies and presents logically their respective positions.

2.0 FUNCTIONAL ORGANIZATION STRUCTURE

2.1 Every organization has a structure, either formal or informal. The newer and smaller the organization, the less formal the structure. As the organization grows, the structure grows with it. Without focus, an organization may take neither on a structure of its own which may not be functional nor in the best interest of the company.

2.2 The Functional Organization Structure is a graphic portrayal of the key functional areas of the company. It represents groupings of functions, not individuals, by major categories as boxes.

2.3 The various levels, from top to bottom, indicate relative levels of authority and responsibility. Lines connecting boxes are basic avenues of communication connecting different authority levels.

2.4 The chart is a valuable tool in depicting and explaining the basic workings of the organization its staff.

3.0 FUNCTIONS

3.1 Each functional area (box) represents a common grouping of functions that need to be performed in that area.

Organization Structure

3.2 The number of functions varies from location to location and from organization to organization. However, a basic core of function will be common to each area, within which the organization functions are categorized and listed.

4.0 POSITION ORGANIZATION CHART

4.1 It naturally follows that people must perform the functions already defined. This provides the nucleus for development of the Position Organization Chart, which depicts position, personnel assigned to these positions, levels of authority and responsibility, channels of communication and reporting relationships, and the potential areas for delegation of authority.

5.0 FLOW OF AUTHORITY

5.1 The President selects and appoints all managers that are necessary for the efficient running of the company, but only to the first level of direct reporting.

5.2 Selected by the function occupant of each box and responsible to each box or function are the individuals of the sub-functions.

5.3 To each supervisor is delegated the authority and responsibility commensurate with the position. This person is thus given authority, responsibility, duties, and "signing off capacity".

5.4 The person's signature also stands as the agreement that the person has accepted the authority allowed, and that the supervisor or manager has granted such authority. This person is fully accountable for performance in his or her area.

5.5 Other individuals in the organization, regardless of their position, who desire input into a function, must work through the head of this function.

5.6 Below each function head are the functions, each the direct responsibility of one and only one, person, selected and appointed by the sub-function head.

# Organization Structure

6.0 LINE OF RESPONSIBILITY

6.1 There is only one line of responsibility in the organization. One person may fulfill more than one function, but one function is responsible to only one other function. **One person cannot serve two masters**.

6.2 Cross-contacts (in the form of cooperation) can be provided for by easily understood agreements between function heads. This permits a member of the organization to cooperate provided only that he/she keeps his/her immediate supervisor informed regarding such contacts. This applies especially to matter for which the function head is held responsible by the person immediately above him/her.

7.0 IMPORTANCE OF DELEGATION

7.1 Good organization requires that the delegation of responsibility be basically complete and that every person in the organization be given the maximum possible autonomy.

7.2 The organization which does not delegate limits its effectiveness to the talents and energies of only a few people.

7.3 By delegating, the company completely utilizes the energies and talents of every member of the organization. Each will be judged by results produced over a period of time and not by a single episode.

7.4 Delegation of responsibility requires equal delegation of authority. An authority means the right to direct, coordinate, and decide, but does not imply autocracy.

7.5 A supervisor's invasion of the area of authority of a subordinate has the effect of relieving the subordinate of responsibility without a definite point for the resumption of responsibility. It brings about confusion and results in a serious loss of productivity.

 **Organization Structure**

8.0 SYNTHESIS OF THE ORGANIZATION CHART

To serve as a guide in reading the chart, and to establish the relative positions between function, the following outline is given:

8.1 **DOWN** the channels (from the top of the chart) flow the directives, responsibilities, policies, and controls which management requires.

8.2 **UP** the channels flow the reports and records which are necessary to keep management informed. These documents communicate the results of operations and insure implementation of directives that have been passed down the line.

8.3 **ORDERS** pass directly through the function which the channels connect. Each function sorts and acts upon them, making decisions and accepting responsibilities involved, passing them down, as needed to lower echelons for action.

8.4 There is no relationship of authority between positions on the same level. There are however, relationships between the functions in the organization, not shown by channels of authority. These relationships have no authority over one another but must be maintained through cooperation and mutual assistance.

9.0 CONCLUSION

9.1 Proper organization will allow the company to grow successfully. As duties are accomplished and positive feedback adjusts for shortcomings or deficiencies, the individual will grow in his or her responsibility.

9.2 Each person knows from whom he or she receives direction and to whom he/she reports. Everyone knows what the company expects, and the standards of performance measures. With these clearly defined duties and responsibilities, each employee can be evaluated and compensated on performance.

 **Organization Structure**

9.3   All personnel must abide by and enforce the functional organization structure. This is a team concept in which each person knows their responsibilities. By using the chain of command properly controlled and work of the organization is properly delegated and controlled.

9.4   When each employee understands and operates within the scope of these organizational principles, far better coordination and cooperation will result. As an additional benefit, better cross training can occur because the duties have been defined and the depth of management has been strengthened.

 **Organization Structure**

Functions in the Organization

Ownership

- Long Term Planning Approval
- Acquisition/Divestment Approval
- Capital Expenditures Approval
- Hire/Discipline CEO

Executive Management

- Mission Statement
- Long Term Planning
- R.O.I.
- Leadership
- Review Operations
- Profit
- Banking Relationships
- Negotiations
- Asset Maintenance
- Budget Forecast & Reviews
- Policy Implementation
- Advisors
- Organization Development
- Public Relations
- Employee Staffing and Compensation
- Cash Management

 **Organization Structure**

Functions in the Organization

Sales and Marketing

- Market Research
- Product Development
- Marketing and Sales Planning
- Pricing and Quotations
- Advertising/Promotions
- Sales Call Backs
- Credit Applications
- Sales Reports
- Customer Service

Operations

- Project Management
- Work Assignments/Scheduling
- Quality Control and Documentation
- Hiring and Disciplining Employees
- Training and Development
- Productivity Monitoring
- Equipment Maintenance
- Technical Services
- Systems Administration

Administration/Finance

- Receipts
- Accounts Payable
- Contract Administration
- Payroll
- General Ledger
- Financial Analysis
- Taxes
- Cash Flow Forecasting

Organization Structure

POSITION ORGANIZATION CHART

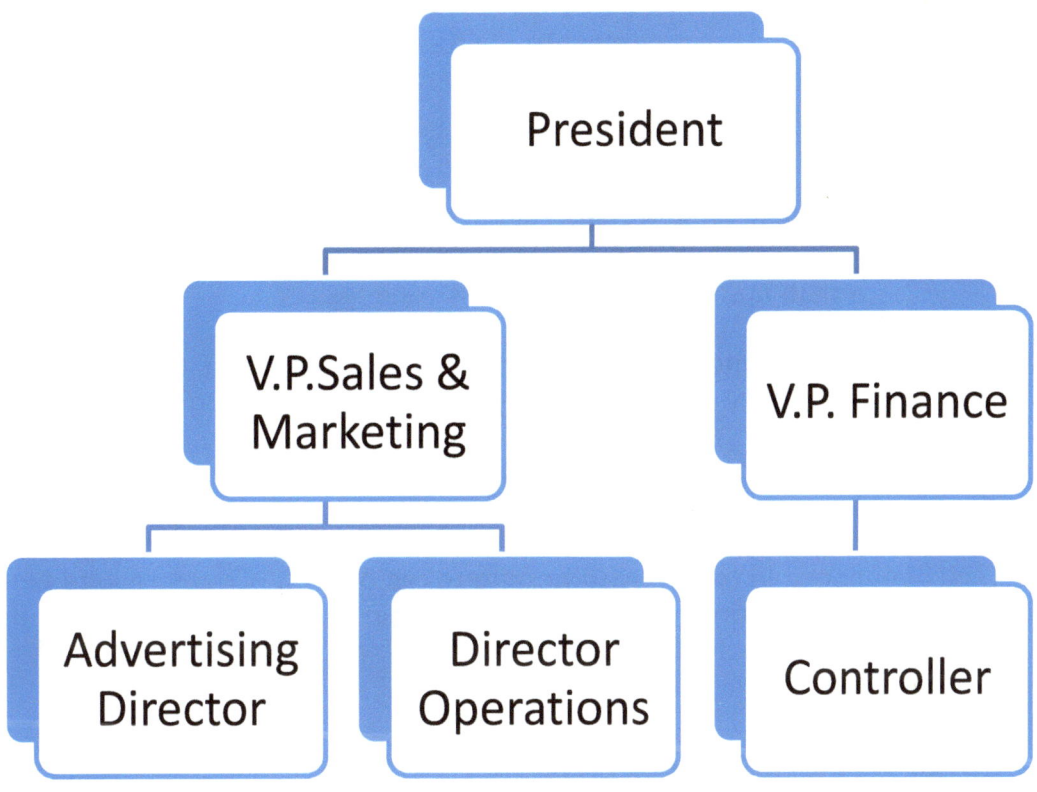

ABC Company, Inc.

Position Organization Chart

Delegation of Authority

1.0   INTRODUCTION

1.1   The purpose of this Standard Procedure is to outline the principles of delegation and describe the method of putting this vital management tool into effect.

Whether or not to delegate is often considered a manager's choice; however in reality, there is not a choice.   At some point, a person's area of responsibility can become greater in scope than a person can physically and mentally handle.

At this point, one must delegate some authority to others in order to properly fulfill all of the responsibilities of his/her position. If one is to be a true manager, delegation is a necessity.

1.2   One of the most basic principles of organization is the delegation of responsibility and accompanying authority. Enough authority must be delegated to ensure that the responsibility can be carried out. This is also one of the most frequently violated principles of organization.

1.3   Employees must be given a direct explanation of who they are responsible to and who he/she takes orders. Chaos results when more than one manager or supervisor begins giving instructions or orders to the same individual as these orders frequently conflict.

2.0   PRINCIPLES OF DELEGATION

2.1   Select a subordinate to whom you will delegate a task. Choose someone who is quite capable of doing this job, and then give that person the authority to do it.

2.2   Clearly communicate the task.

The manager and subordinate should agree on the following:
2.2.1   The scope of the task
2.2.2   Specific results to be achieved
2.2.3   Clarity of the relative importance of the task
2.2.4   A time schedule that provides not only a deadline for the completion of the task but specifies checkpoints along the way as well.
2.2.5   The necessary authority to carry out the job.
2.2.6   A pre-determined way to measure results.

 **Delegation of Authority**

2.3   Delegate the good and the bad.

        If you just give others the undesirable tasks, you will retard their
        motivation, commitment and development. Delegate interesting,
        rewarding and challenging jobs as well as mundane tasks.

2.4   Delegate gradually.

        Do not transfer too many responsibilities at one time.

2.5   Delegate in advance.

        Do not wait until a crisis is in effect to delegate.

2.6   Inform all affected people and departments.

        This to eliminate confusion and to help maintain cohesiveness in the
        operation of the department. When you assign a task, be sure that
        everyone knows that this individual has the responsibility and
        authority to complete the job.

2.7   Let the subordinate manage.

        Delegate for specific results and let the individual decide how to go
        about doing the job.

2.8   Follow-up.

        Make sure that you follow up and give the person constructive
        feedback on the results attained.

2.9   Remain consistent.

        Keep your expectations consistent with the original agreed – upon
        results. If changes occur discuss them openly with the individual.

2.10   Review in private surroundings.

        Should the results be less than desirable, review them in private with
        the individual and teach how he or she could have improved the
        results.

Delegation of Authority

3.0   DELEGATION

3.1   Delegation of authority may be divided into three categories as follow:

    3.1.1   Total Authority – The individual <u>may take action</u> without notifying anyone for approval.

    3.1.2   Partial Authority – Supervisor retains veto power, and the individual <u>may take action only after securing approval</u> of the action

    3.1.3   Limited Authority – The individual can develop actions to be taken and <u>make recommendation, but cannot take action.</u>

3.2   What to delegate? Divide your responsibilities and duties into three categories as follow:

    3.2.1   Relatively Unimportant routine duties and tasks.

    These are items where a bad decision will not be costly and can be reversed with minimal consequences.

    Label these "A" items

    3.2.2   Fairly important tasks and duties.

    These are items were your experience and expertise may be required and although errors and mistakes may be most costly, they will not be disastrous.

    Label these "B" items

    3.2.3   Critically important

    Those items where an error in judgment or poor decision will be very costly.

    Label these "C" items

3.3   Delegate all of your "A" items.

3.4   Delegate some of your "B" items.

3.5   Delegate all tasks that cannot be completed under a time constraint.

Delegation of Authority

3.6 Retain all of your "C" items. Those responsibilities that require your personal handling.

4.0 AUTHORITY

4.1 In order for a subordinate to accomplish a task, he/she has to be given a certain amount of authority. Remember that authority can be delegated, but it is still your responsibility to see that the task is accomplished.

4.2 Your goal is to have the subordinate develop a plan of action, and then be able to trust his/her ability to make the proper choice in keeping with his/her ability and take the appropriate actions to implement the decision.

4.3 Pont out to subordinates any policies and procedures that they should be aware of. Put these or any other instruction in writing. Reference can always be made to a written copy.

Remember, very few people can remember everything that is said and remember it in the correct context.

5.0 MAINTAINING CONTROL

5.1 When you manage through others, it is vital that you keep control. You do this by holding a subordinate accountable to you for their actions and checking their progress and /or results along the way.

Therefore in delegating authority to subordinates, you must strike a balance in controlling them. While you do not want to interfere, you must be kept informed of progress and results. This should be accomplished through reports and/or meetings.

5.1.1 Reports must provide you with the right information at the right time to be of value.

5.1.2 Periodic meetings held with your subordinates will allow for interaction between them as well as comments on activities, accomplishments, problems and opportunities.

Delegation of Authority

6.0 COACHING YOUR STAFF

6.1 Delegation does not end with good control. It involves teaching and learning management skills at all levels. This is a never ending process and must be approached as such. It is essential within any organization that this process continues for the organization to prosper.

6.2 **It is also essential to keep your subordinates informed and give them the facts they need in order to make intelligent and timely decisions.**

Delegation of authority can only be effective when you have good communications. Convey your thinking to your subordinates as much as you can in writing, and ask questions to make sure a total understanding has been reached.

6.2.1 Never leave your staff with instructions that are specific enough to only be done one way. You will be surprised at both how much more cooperation you will receive, and at the probable suggestion(s) as to how the task may be more successfully accomplished.

7.0 ALLOW YOUR STAFF TO FUNCTION

7.1 Selecting competent people, defining their authority, maintaining control, and coaching set the stage for success. Now let your staff do what you told them they could do. Let them make mistakes! It is a very educational principle, (and remembers that the mistakes made, will only be on the non-critical items).

7.2 It is also vitally important to let competent subordinates perform in their own style rather that insisting that they do things as you would have done them. Judge your subordinates on their results, not only on their methods.

7.3 Once having given an employee the authority to act, your next concern should be that their actions conform to established policies and procedures. If subordinates wish to proceed otherwise, they must demonstrate to you that a change in the policy or procedure is necessary. If you agree, the change must be instituted before the subordinate initiates the action involved.

Delegation of Authority

7.4   If a subordinate does well, tell him/her. Far too often we jump at the chance to criticize and take for granted tasks that are done well. Criticism has its place, but so do compliments. Both are very important in building and developing managers within your organization. Remember to keep adding value.

Learning is important. It takes time, and it must be adapted to the duties and skills within the company. The company can imitate other company philosophies and practices, but execution of the policies and procedures is the most important ingredient. And remember, successful execution skills are acquired only through practice and constant nurturing.

 **Position Guide Development**

1.0 INTRODUCTION

1.1 The purpose of this Standard Procedure is to outline the use and development of position guides for the personnel in the company. There should be a written guide for every management and supervisory position in the company.

1.2 Position Guides are written to clarify and document the specific authorities, responsibilities, duties, and standards of performance for each key job in the company. They ensure that ownership's expectations are communicated, as no one can perform to expectations unless they clearly understand them.

1.3 The position guides provide the basis for performance evaluations. An individual is evaluated by comparing actual performance to the responsibilities, duties and standards of performance listed in the guide.

2.0 DRAFTING THE POSITION GUIDE

2.1 It is helpful to get employee assistance in developing the guides. They provide valuable insight into the positions, and seeking their input will increase their commitment to perform within the specified guidelines. Keep in mind that the guides must follow the functional positions illustrated in the Positional Organization Chart, and are not normally negotiated or tailored to the individuals in those positions.

2.2 Position Guidelines will be written in this format:

2.2.1 <u>Introduction</u> – A brief paragraph stating the name of the position and the company.

2.2.2 <u>Functional Role</u> – This shall include a sentence or short paragraph to describe the overall impact the position has on the company.

2.2.3 <u>Physical Requirements</u> – This is an overview of the specific physical demands of the position as required by several national laws. The U.S. Federal Americans with Disabilities Act of 1989 states that any company must make "reasonable accommodations" for individuals qualified for the position and no person shall be rejected simply because of a physical or mental challenge.

Position Guide Development

2.2.4   <u>Reporting Relationship</u> – Indicate to what position this job reports (use the title of the position, not the individual's name). Also indicate the titles of any position that report directly to this position.

2.2.5   <u>Authority</u> – This is the power to take action with prescribed limitations without obtaining prior approval. List the authorities and limitations of this position.

2.2.6   <u>Responsibilities</u> – Responsibilities are not necessarily what the individual does, but rather that which he or she must ensure is accomplished. The responsibilities must be results-oriented, not task oriented.

2.2.7   <u>Principal Duties</u> – List the specific tasks and duties that must be performed to accomplish the responsibilities of the position. It is sometimes difficult to distinguish a task from a responsibility; this does not matter as long as the individual realizes it is his/her responsibility.

2.2.8   <u>Measures of Performance</u> – These must be the specific and if possible, quantifiable measurement criteria used to evaluate the performance of the employee. This will focus the employee's efforts on listed criteria. Make sure the standards cover all the key functions of the position.

2.2.9   <u>Acknowledgment</u> – State that the position guides has been reviewed and is understood. It is signed by the manager and the employee receiving the guide and then filed in the employee's personnel file, with a copy being provided to the employee.

2.3   Position guides must be regularly reviewed and revised. Annual reviews are recommended. Job duties, authorities, and responsibilities will change over time and position guides need to be modified accordingly. All revised guides must be dated, signed and filed in each employee's personnel record.

 **Position Guide Development**

3.0   FINALIZING THE POSITION GUIDE

3.1   The Position Guide will be drafted by the manager which directly supervises the position. Before each guide is distributed, the owner must approve it. The approved guide must be carefully reviewed with the employee in that position. It is essential that each employee clearly understand what is expected of him or her, what their goals are, and how to achieve them.

 **Hiring Procedure**

1.0   INTRODUCTION

1.1   This procedure is a general guideline for finding the best qualified employees for the company.

1.2   The responsibility for hiring is in the hands of the Supervisor and must be consistent throughout the organization.

2.0   POSITION APPROVAL AND ADVERTISING

2.1   A job description (or task sheet) with personnel specifications and salary range must be set for a position before beginning the hiring process. The immediate supervisor will prepare the job description/task sheet for approval by the President, and may suggest a salary range for a new title.

2.2   An approved job opening should be posted on the company bulletin board for one week before the job is advertised to the public. This gives current employees a first chance to seek advancement in the company. It also allow for your personal network and bounty system to work.

2.3   Advertise the position using newspaper, radio, and/or the Internet outside the company if no qualified internal candidates come forward within a reasonable time. Use schools, churches, fitness centers, suppliers, employment agencies or government placement agencies to find potential candidates.

3.0   SELECTING PEOPLE TO INTERVIEW

3.1   A standard employment application should be used and revised on a continuing basis to keep it in compliance with regulation. The admissibility of questions such as marital status and convictions should be addressed to the State Department of Labor to find out what are the current rulings. In addition, do not let the pay expected cloud your judgment on an applicant.

3.2   Before any part of the interview process begins, you must have a completed application, even if a resume has been provided. (It collects the same information about every candidate in the same format). Some resumes omit information you may want.

Hiring Procedure

3.3   It is advisable to retain all job application for at least 90 days.

3.4   When a completed application is returned, it must be checked to ensure that all information has been provided. If information is missing, contact the candidate to complete the information.

3.5   The qualifications for the job determine how much experience a person will need. Look for candidate that "on paper" has the qualification you want and arrange to interview them.

3.6   There are several methods of screening multiple candidates. The best method depends on the job.

        3.6.1   In the ad, listing a telephone number instead of an address permits you to screen all candidates initially by telephone, if you only have time for a few in-person interviews. Screen the calls by asking about principal skills and experience, to bring in only a few top candidates.

        3.6.2   To select from a pool of similar workers, you might call them all in at once to explain the job to the whole group, and then carry out brief individual questioning. This is very rapid but requires all of the candidates to be physically present.

3.7   Information on all applications should be verified as a safeguard against misrepresentation on the application. Under no circumstances should you hire anyone who has provided false information on an application. Therefore, it is crucial to verify the information before the applicant is hired.

3.8   It is extremely important to verify any licensing or certification information such as driving record for appropriate positions.

4.0   AVOIDING DISCRIMINATION IN INTERVIEWING

4.1   All aspects of the hiring process should be free of references to topics that an applicant could take to court as discrimination. Some of the major issues are discussed here.

4.2   The Age Discrimination regulations are intended to prohibit discrimination on the basis of age for individuals between 40 and 64. Asking questions about age could be construed as unlawful.

# Hiring Procedure

4.3 Arrest records provide no indication of guilt. Be sure to ask about convictions.

4.4 As with arrest records, asking about credit records, owning or renting a home and owning a car, and a record of wage garnishments my unlawful discriminate against minorities or women, who historically have less access to credit.

4.5 Height, weight, eye and hair color are personal characteristics related to race and gender, and are not relevant to most jobs. Phrase questions in terms of abilities, not appearance.

4.6 Marital status, children under 18, maiden name, gender and indicating Mr. Mrs. or Ms. Are not necessary questions. Companies have been successfully sued for refusing to hire a married woman, paying a married woman less than a man (because here income is a "second income") or distinguishing between men with children and women with children. Additionally, some minorities have higher rates of divorce or number of children, and could sue for discrimination on the basis of race, religion or national origin.

4.7 The policies discussed above relate to equal opportunity statues, requiring that all employees be given an equal chance at a job, promotion or employment benefit without regard to personal characteristics. The two major types of discrimination are "disparate treatment", intentional discrimination against a class of people.

4.8 This is not an exhaustive review of regulations, as both federal and provincial regulations are in a constant state of change. Consult your local labor law references for further information.

5.0 INTERVIEWING

5.1 The interviewer must come prepared to an interview with three things.

1. The job description or task sheet.

2. A list of "Open Questions" (Questions which start with the words "Why" What""When" Where" "How" "Who" and "Tell Me") to ask or topics to cover with all candidates. Ask the same questions of everyone. You do not have to ask them in the same order, but you should cover the some ground with each person.

Hiring Procedure

3. A score sheet listing what you are looking for in an outstanding candidate for the position, which you will complete to compare the candidates by category and total scores.

5.2   You need two levels of information in evaluating a candidate.

    5.2.1   Skills, education and experience. The employment application should help you evaluate the candidate's measurable qualifications, but you should go over this information in person just in case their description of work is different from yours. For example, they may have directed other workers from time to time, but they may not be fully experienced supervisors.

    5.2.2   Motivation and positive attitude. These are qualifications that are difficult to identify except through specific work examples or from personal references. Look carefully for signs that the person may be a problem later on. You do not have to hire someone who will not meet your company's standards for quality and teamwork.

        5.2.2.1   Is the candidate trainable, willing to follow directions, a hard worker? Ask for examples of what they learned and how they feel about learning new things; for how they handle unexpected situations (did they consult with their boss). If no one is looking over their shoulder, what do they do?

        5.2.2.2   If specific examples do not help you make your decision, you may find it useful to try direct questions such as:

"Why did you choose this line of work? What about it do you like now?"

"Tell me five characteristics that describe you as a worker?"

"Why do you want to leave your present job?" "

"What do you want in a job that you are not getting now?"

Hiring Procedure

5.3   Be enthusiastic and positive during the interview. You represent the company to this person, and you must project a positive image. You do not want a candidate you have selected to turn you down! However, do not over sell the company or the position, no matter how much you need to fill the position. If the candidate has an inflated perception of the position or the working conditions, it will cause dissatisfaction and possible turnover when they begin work.

5.4   Let the candidate ask questions. Decide what you want every candidate to know and what you do not wish to discuss. They probably would like to know if the company is growing, what the hours are, and other job-related questions.

5.5   If the applicant volunteers any personal facts related to information discussed above, interrupt them and remind them that the interview is confined to job-related information and that only that information will be use in the final hiring decision.

5.6   Clearly state the next step in the selection process for the candidate. Close an interview with a handshake, even if it did not go well.

5.7   Contact at least one reference for any candidate that you are considering seriously, to get confirmation of their abilities and professionalism. Speak to a former supervisor, not a personnel department whenever possible.

   5.7.1   Some employers will be reluctant to give candid opinions about a former employee, and will only confirm facts such as dates of an employee's employment period. There is some concern that employees may sue the former employer if their failure to find a job was due to a poor reference.

   5.7.2   Even for such employers, if you read between the lines, your questions should turn up some information about the candidate's performance.

   5.7.3   Questioning references should include the basics:

          Confirm the job title and employment period.
          Ask about attendance, initative, overall performance.
          Ask if they would hire the person right now. This can be a very revealing question.

 # Hiring Procedure

5.8   Rate each candidate on how well you believe they would perform the primary duties of the job based on their qualifications ant trainability. Select the person whom you believe will exceed the performance requirements of the job. Hire the best!

5.9   Determine when the candidate can start work, and prepare an orientation for their first few days of work. Very often candidates will not be available immediately due to a desire to provide their current employer with sufficient notice of resignation. No matter how much you need to fill a position, do not let the availability eliminate your top candidate in favor of one not as qualified. If a candidate is concerned about giving notice to their current employer, they will probably treat you with the same respect.

6.0   ORIENTATION

6.1   When a new employee is hired, there should be a short orientation to the company, including:

       6.1.1   Completion of new hire paperwork.

       6.1.2   Review and acknowledgement of the Employee Handbook and other policies.

       6.1.3   Introduction to management and co-workers.

       6.1.4   Assignment of personnel responsible for training.

7.0   CONCLUSION

7.1   In a small organization you are looking for people who are flexible and willing to make things happen as supportive team players.

7.2   In advertising, interviewing, and conducting performance reviews, always stick to objective job-related issues. By all means, avoid the hot topics.

Hiring Procedure

7.3 The primary benefit to be realized from having hiring guidelines in place is establishing consistency. The company now has (or will have in the near future) various management personnel involved in interviewing and selecting candidates for open position.

7.4 In addition, candidates that are subjected to a professional, positive interview and hiring process will become productive sooner and probably stay longer.

7.5 By adhering to the guidelines presented, you will reduce exposure to grievances or litigation relating to misunderstanding or discrimination.

 **Performance Evaluations**

1.0 YOUR RESPONSIBILITIES

Appraisals: "The systematic description of an individual's job relevant strengths and weaknesses."

1.1 Appraising your employees' performance is one of your most important responsibilities as a manager and it will be one of your most difficult jobs. As you will learn from this operating procedure, the appraisal program is a critical link in a series of steps that move us toward company goals and objectives.

1.2 You are responsible for ensuring all employees in the Company's organization structure receive an appraisal quarterly. You are also responsible for the quality of those appraisals.

2.0 WHY APPRAISALS?

2.1 We conduct employee performance appraisals in order to:

2.1.1 Communicate company goals and objectives.

2.1.2 Ensure consistent treatment of all employees.

2.1.3 Ensure fair treatment for everyone, and

2.1.4 Identify training and development needs.

2.2 An appraisal is the time for a formal discussion of individual performance relating to company goals and objectives. Everyone's performance is guided by a carefully designed schedule of duties (a job description or task sheet). Management ensures everyone's collective efforts move toward our goals and objectives. As much as possible, standards or measurements of performance have been incorporated into these job descriptions. Not only do the employees know what is to be done, but they also understand how well it is to be done.

2.3 An appraisal is not a personality assessment. It is an objective discussion concerning performance to expectation. The phrase is worth repeating: **"Performance to Expectations!"**

 **Performance Evaluations**

3.0 WHAT PRECEDES THE APPRAISAL PROCESS?

3.1 From the above introduction, the answer to this question should be obvious. An appraisal can only be conducted after the employee has an understanding of your expectations. After all, if the appraisal judges performance to expectations, how can it proceed without a clear understanding of those expectations?

3.2 Step 1 in the appraisal process then is...

3.2.1 The job description or task sheet.

3.2.3 Daily appraisals! All employees deserve frequent feedback on their performance to your expectations. No surprises! Keep notes.

3.3 Most appraisals should be routine...if you have supported the employee with frequent feedback. Your job performance demands feedback. It is a poor supervisor who fears an immediate response to a performance problem, wanting to wait for the "safety" of time and the formal appraisal interview. If you have done your job, the employee already knows how you will evaluate their performance. They will not be surprised by what you have to say. As important as frequent feedback is, keeping notes of that feedback is more vital to an effective appraisal. Your memory is not going to be sufficient when it comes time to compose your evaluation. Keep a working file on each employee, a record containing examples of his or her performance. When you are through with the notes in your working file (presumably after they have been recorded on the appraisal form), properly discard them.

3.4 These procedures on record keeping have been developed to ensure consistent, fair treatment of all employees.

4.0 WHAT TYPE OF APPRAISAL DO WE USE?

4.1 There are a number of different types of appraisals, all of them proven effective in many business settings. An appraisal method should have these characteristics:

Performance Evaluations

4.1.1 Relevance – A clear link between the performance standards for a particular job and our company goals.

4.1.2 Sensitivity – It is capable of distinguishing effective from ineffective performers.

4.1.3 Reliability -   In this context, we refer to consistency of judgment. Appraisals made by raters working independently of one another should agree closely.

4.1.4 Acceptability – The method must have the support of those who will use it.

4.1.5 Practicality - It is easy for managers and employees to understand and use.

5.0   THE APPRAISAL PROCESS, ONE STEP AT A TIME

5.1   **Schedule all your appraisals.** Actually put them on your calendar. There are no guidelines as to how many you can conduct on one day. Do what makes sense for you and your employees.

5.2   **The employee completes his/her own appraisal form.** A few days before the scheduled appraisal give the employee an appraisal form and ask him/her to complete it and return it to you by a given date. Make sure at this time he/she understands how to complete the form. Explain to employees that it is important that both you and they give some thought to their performance during the past three months. In this manner, the appraisal can be done quickly and effectively. Remind them specific examples are important, and required if they rate their performance at either extreme ("Outstanding" or "Unsatisfactory").

5.3   **Complete your own draft form on the employee**. Do this before you see the employee's completed form. You will be much more effective in your evaluation if both you and the employee complete a form independently. Pull out your working file on the employee (not the company official personnel file) for reminders about specific examples you have noted during this appraisal period.

 **Performance Evaluations**

5.4 **Get the employee's self-appraisal and set a date for the appraisal meeting**. Make sure the date you set is convenient for both you and the employee.

5.5 **Compare the employee's self-appraisal with your draft.** Look for areas of agreement and disagreement, and then prepare for the appraisal meeting based on these areas. The meeting will move quickly if you know which performance areas you agree on – not as much time needs to be spent on them.

5.6 **Complete an appraisal form on the employee.** The self-appraisal you received from the employee may have changed your mind on certain performance areas. While you should not accept the employee's evaluation simply to avoid conflict, do not be afraid to change your mind either. If the employee has given you some good example to support their position, then perhaps your appraisal should change. If there is disagreement and the employee has not given you examples, then you should be prepared to cite examples of your own.

5.7 **Hqld the Interview.** There will be more on this later, but at the end of the interview make sure you get the employee's comments and signature on the appraisal form.

5.8 **Put the appraisal in the employee's personnel file.**

6.0 THE APPRAISAL MEETING

6.1 The day has arrived and you are about to face the employee with a very difficult subject: **how you rate their performance**. Most of us work so closely with our employees we have developed a friendship with them. Discussing strengths and weaknesses becomes and especially trying experience. There are a few keys to a successful appraisal meeting and you should review them before every such interview. None however are as important as the first one.

6.1.1. **Be Prepared!** There is no substitute for good preparation, including those performance notes you should have been compiling during the past three months. Review them now and practice the carefully chosen words you intend to use to explain your appraisal. Be prepared also to explain the meaning of the company's appraisal process and its importance to everyone's success.

Performance Evaluations

6.1.2 Reserve a quiet place and choose an appropriate time. There is nothing worse you can do than accept an interruption during the appraisal interview or set a time when you, or the employee is distracted by worries over time. Never be late for this meeting. Choose a time when all of this is possible.

6.1.3 Set the tone in the first few seconds. A relaxed atmosphere is best for this appraisal meeting. If you think it may help calm you or the employee, begin the interview by talking about something interesting. When people are tense or feel threatened, they put up barriers hindering their ability to listen. After the atmosphere is relaxed, get down to business and bring the focus back to the employee's goals and objectives. A relaxed atmosphere does not mean a circus atmosphere!

6.1.4 Begin with the best. It is generally best to begin the appraisal with some good news. Do not be concerned about skipping around the appraisal form. There is no required pattern to the discussion.

6.1.5 Never overreact to an employee's anger. Anger results from fear, frustration and disappointment. If you remain calm and listen. The atmosphere will probably "discharge" and the employee will begin to lose the fear, frustration or disappointment that triggered their anger. If the meeting deteriorates, call a halt to it and tell him/her this is not a good time for the discussion. Reschedule it for a few days in the future and let him/her know you are looking forward to a positive discussion at that time.

6.1.6 Encourage the employee's participation. She/he should have a perception of, and a feeling that his/her ideas are genuinely welcomed. Participation encourages the belief the appraisal was a constructive activity.

6.1.7 Be specific and use examples. Not only do examples and illustrations help focus the appraisal on constructive dialogue, but they also show that you have knowledge of the employee's performance. Examples mean you have cared enough about the employee to carefully observe their performance. They show you want the employee to succeed.

Performance Evaluations

6.1.8 **Be an active listener.** Communicate verbally and non-verbally (e.g. by maintaining eye contact). Do not interrupt. Watch for verbal as well as nonverbal clues regarding the employee's agreement or disagreement. Stop often to summarize what has been said and agreed upon.

7.0   SPECIAL PROBLEMS

7.1   **Special Reporting Periods**. Unfortunately it is sometimes necessary to elevate the nature of an unsatisfactory appraisal. When an employee consistently performs unsatisfactorily, formal action may be the answer to improved performance.

7.2   **Refusal to Sign.** Sometimes, but rarely and usually only with a poor appraisal, an employee will be reluctant to sign the appraisal.

The employee must sign all appraisals!

You have a problem if they refuse to sign the form. First you should solicit the employee's written comments and remind them their signature on the form does not mean they agree with the appraisal, only that they have received it.

The employee's written comments are not restricted in either content or form. For instance, the employee may write, "I do not agree with this appraisal" and the fell free to sign it.

If the employee still refuses to sign the form, quickly review the areas in which you both agree. Narrow down the areas of disagreement so agreement might still be possible. At this point you should clearly understand the employee's position, is that position supported by examples? Is your differing position also supported by examples?

No productive purpose is served by a refusal to compromise.

Maybe you can agree to concede the employee's wishes as long as she/he is willing to accept a training and development plan that addresses your comparative dissatisfaction.

 **Performance Evaluations**

8.0   COMMON ERRORS

8.1   Halo Effect. This is the most pervasive error in performance appraisals. Raters who commit this error assign their rating on the basis of global (either good or bad) impressions or employees. An employee is rated either high or low on many areas of job performance because the evaluator knows (or thinks he/she knows) the employees is high or low on some specific aspect. The "Halo Evaluator" has forgotten to "wipe the slate clean" with every new performance area.

For instance: If an employee displays intelligence by employing an exceptional vocabulary, he/she must also learn new assignments quickly; if a female employee is pretty, she must also be good with customer service; the best worker in terms of completing daily assignments must also be the most accurate.

8.2   Contrast Error. These result when several employees are compared to each other rather that to an objective standard of performance. If, say, the first two employees are unsatisfactory, while the third is actually average, the third employee may well be rated outstanding because in contrast to the first two, his/her "average" level of job performance is magnified. Likewise, "average" performance could be unfairly downgraded if the first few workers are outstanding.

8.3   Recent Error. These result when supervisors assign ratings on the basis of the employee's most recent performance. It is most likely to occur when appraisal are done only after long periods.

9.0   SUMMARY

Conducting performance appraisal is a very important job. It is your means of effectively communicating company goals and objectives. Through the job description, you have carefully designed each employee's duties so the combined effort of all employees will move the company towards its objectives. The performance appraisal interview is your time to answer the employee's question:

"So, Boss, how am I doing in performing to your expectations?"

Performance Evaluations
Employee Performance Appraisal

(Administrative Manager)

Employee Name_____ Title_____

Employment Date_____ Time in Position_____ Years_____ Months_____ Employee Payroll #_____

The Employee performing the requirements of the Job herein is required to complete the Duties and Tasks consistently, accurately, timely, safely, and at the lowest feasible cost. Furthermore, other performance criteria are to be met. Performance of the stated Job Criteria shall be Rated according to the following Scale:

Definitions of Performance Ratings

O – **Outstanding** – Performance is exceptional in all areas and is recognized as being far superior to others.

V – **Very Good** – Results clearly exceed most position requirements. Performance is of high quality and is achieved on a continual basis.

G – **Good** – Competent and dependable level of performance. Most performance standards of the job.

I - **Improvement Needed** – Performance is deficient in certain areas. Improvement is necessary.

U – **Unsatisfactory** – Results are generally unacceptable and require immediate improvement. No merit increase should be granted to an individual with this rating.

N/A – **Not applicable** or too soon to rate.

Responsibility, Duty or Tasks	Rating	Scale	Supporting Details or Comments
1.The full monthly financial statements including	O ☐	100-90	Points
P &L's, A/P Aging Reports are prepared and	V ☐	89-80	☐
Completed accurately by the 5th of the month.	G ☐	79-70	
	I ☐	69-60	
	U ☐	Below 60	
2.Cash Flow Projections and Key Indicator Reports	O ☐	100-90	Points
are presented weekly to the President on Monday	V ☐	89-80	☐
morning.	G ☐	79-70	
	I ☐	69-60	
	U ☐	Below 60	

Performance Evaluations

Responsibility, Duty or Tasks	Rating		Scale	Supporting Details or Comments
3.Invoices are complete and accurate so that no delays occur in receipt of funds.	O	☐	100-90	Points ☐
	V	☐	89-80	
	G	☐	79-70	
	I	☐	69-60	
	U	☐	Below 60	
4.Monthly Variance Report is presented by the 5th day of each month.	O	☐	100-90	Points ☐
	V	☐	89-80	
	G	☐	79-70	
	I	☐	69-60	
	U	☐	Below 60	

Rate employees overall performance in comparison to policies and procedures along with each job description

Total Points ☐ Number of Factors Rated ☐ = Weighted Score ☐

Complete all of the following section:

1. Accomplishments or new abilities demonstrated since last review _____

_____

2. Specific areas of needed improvements_____

_____

Additional Employee Comments:_____

_____

Discussed with individual on ____/____/_____   Employee's Supervisor_____

Follow-up requested/desired? [ ]Yes [ ]No

Employee's Signature_____   Date Signed_____

Progressive Discipline

1.0 PROGRESSIVE DISCIPLINE

1.1 Counterproductive behavior and the reluctance or inability of supervisor with the company to effectively and consistently deal with it is a serious problem for management. This type of behavior is serious because it contributes to **LOW MORALE** and **REDUCED PRODUCTIVITY**. The cost of this behavior is very high, with significant impact on the bottom-line profits.

1.2 In order to achieve and consistently maintain a good climate of employee relations, all supervisors need the tools to do the job, and must understand the nature of the disciplinary process…what is, how it functions and the consequences if appropriate and prompt actions are not taken.

2.0 WHY SUPERVISORS DO NOT DISCIPLINE

2.1 Some of the reasons why disciplinary action is not taken on a consistent basis are as follows:

2.1.1 Lack of Training: Some supervisors do not know how to administer discipline effectively and, therefore, lack the confidence to tackle the problem.

2.1.2 Management Will Not Back Me Up: This fear probably reflects past experience and may have some truth. If the facts are correct and actions appropriate, disciplinary action will usually be supported by higher management.

2.1.3 Fear of Consequences: There have been cases of retaliation against the supervisor in the form of threats or physical damage against the supervisor or his/her property.

2.1.4 Other Supervisors Do Not: Why should I take action, stick my neck out, when others do not seem to care or are afraid?

2.1.5 I Do Not Have the Time: Fact finding, interviewing the parties involved, the investigation process, all take time, which I do not have enough of already.

2.1.6 Guilt Feelings: Some supervisors are guilty of the same kind of conduct at one time or another and feel guilty about disciplining someone else.

 **Progressive Discipline**

      2.1.7 <u>Loss of Friendship:</u> Disciplinary action may cause loss of friendship and alienation from members of the work group.

      2.1.8 <u>Dislike of Conflict:</u> Some people will avoid confronting a difficult situation, especially if it involves interpersonal conflict.

      2.1.9 <u>Desire to be a "Nice Guy":</u> I will get more work and loyalty from my work group if they like me. Some people confuse being liked with being respected.

3.0   COUNTERPRODUCTIVE BEHAVIORS

3.1   We will identify types of employee behavior which are barriers to efficient performance. These behaviors represent a significant cost to the company. Decreasing such counterproductive activities through better supervision, maintenance of positive discipline and appropriate action programs will contribute to more successful operations. The most common counterproductive activities by employees include:

      3.1.1 <u>Absenteeism:</u> While some absences are obviously legitimate and preventable, many are not. A well-devised follow-up program can reduce absenteeism at considerable cost savings to the company.

      3.1.2 <u>Poor Quality:</u> Below standard quality identifies itself in two way: Product rejected and scrapped (from typed reports to damaged product) or in service complaints by customers. The latter is more serious since it may lead to extra costs and to permanent loss from sales to that customer.

3.2   There are obviously more factors which contribute to inefficiency, but counterproductive activities are a reality and represent a high cost to the company. All of the activities mentioned, to a significant degree can be controlled or their impact lessened by effective supervision.

3.3   A work environment that maintains a high degree of morale, well trained employees who cooperatively work together to achieve the objectives of the group will have a minimum of counterproductive employee behavior. In specific instances where such activities exist beyond acceptable limits, the use of a Progress Discipline System is appropriate and necessary for the company and the well being of the other employees.

Progressive Discipline

3.2.1 <u>Accidents:</u>   Research evidence indicates a direct relationship between accidents and employee dissatisfaction on the job. Safety violations or careless act, of either in an office environment or on the road, may lead to disciplinary action. It is, therefore, appropriate for us to include accidents in our list to counterproductive activities.

3.2.2. <u>Inventory Shrinkage:</u> While some shrinkage of material and product can be attributed to other varied causes, our concern is for that which can be related to theft, carelessness or faulty record keeping.

3.2.3 <u>Machine/Equipment Repair:</u> Machines and equipment do wear out. They need preventive maintenance and repair. In addition to normal breakdown, however, they experience sabotage, neglect from indifference or careless abuse (it is not mine syndrome). This activity can be very costly, not only in repair cost, but in reduced levels of productivity and safety.

3.3   In addition to the problems mentioned in 3.1, there are other types of employee behavior which are disruptive, destructive, or both. These require immediate attention by the supervisor, either through positive behavior change strategies such as suspension, or where necessary, termination. Examples include insubordination, falsification of work records, fighting, theft, drinking, use of drugs, etc.

3.4   Good management stresses a positive approach in the effective work force. Unfortunately, fear of punishment is still the most effective deterrent understood by some employees. Permissiveness, laxness, and negligence on the part of supervision to apply rules may be license for some to take advantage of the situation. In such cases, determination to exercise firm discipline may be the only remaining remedy. On the other hand, when employees understand and accept rules which they consider sensible and fair, they become built-in regulators of employee conduct and reduce the negative impact of counterproductive behavior.

3.5   **DISCIPLINE!** - "Treatment which corrects or punishes behavior".

3.5.1 Unfortunately, discipline is frequently thought of in this narrow and punitive sense.

 **Progressive Discipline**

3.5.2 When discipline is synonymous with punishment, it is entirely negative.

3.5.3 Discipline can also be defined as **"CONSTRUCTIVE, POSITIVE FORCE** that enables people to work together in harmony."

3.6 To a work group, discipline should mean that each member knows his or her job well and works cooperatively with the group to carry out assignments and achieve the goals of the group in a timely manner.

3.7 **A PROGRESSIVE DISCIPLINE PROGRAM** provides a stepped procedure for discipline. The procedure meets arbitrator tests for Due Process and Just Cause and has successfully met all challenges in both arbitration and court proceedings.

3.8 The purpose of **PROGRESSIVE DISCIPLINE** is to correct the employee's behavior and restore the person to a state within the group and to deter other employees from being tempted to do the same or similar kinds of acts. The supervisor's actions serve as a constraint upon future individual or group behavior of a negative nature.

4.0 KEY FACTORS

4.1 In analyzing discipline problems, no two situations are quite the same. This creates some stress and uncertainty in how to proceed in a case where discipline may be called for. Supervisors would find a great deal of comfort in having a simple formula to apply to any and all circumstances.

Realistically, however, life and people are infinitely more complex and the situation variables are many. Therefore, the supervisor must carefully investigate and thoroughly consider these key factors in arriving at the degree of penalty and the course of action in a disciplinary case.

4.1.1 Seriousness of the Problem: Is it a major infraction requiring immediate action, or suspension while the investigation is conducted?

4.1.2 Time Span: Has this or other infractions been caused lately by the same employee?

# Progressive Discipline

4.1.3 <u>Frequency of the Same Problem:</u> Is the incident one of a recurring pattern or behavior? Is it minor in nature, or a major infraction?

4.1.4 <u>Past Practices:</u> This is a crucial area. How has the company handled similar situation in the past?

4.1.5 <u>Employee Work History:</u> Is the employee normally a cooperative worker? How long has he/she been with the company? What has been the quality of performance? How is his/her physical and emotional health?

4.1.6 <u>Extenuating Circumstances:</u> Are there unusual factors which have contributed to the situation?

4.1.7 <u>Clearly Defined Rules:</u> Are rules governing employee conduct clearly defined and communicated to employees and can all employees be reasonably expected to know them?

4.2 Our progressive discipline program is based on the following guidelines:

4.2.1 The Rules are Reasonable.

4.2.2 The rules reflect the needs of the company to efficiently sell its products and serve the customer.

4.2.3 The rules will be discussed with employees to insure that each employee understands them and the reasons for them.

4.2.4 The rules pertain to the work place. They do not restrict the lives of employees, except for matters which might be serious enough to adversely affect our business or the reputation of the company in the community.

4.2.5 Rules must be consistently enforced. Infractions should be dealt with fairly and punishment given uniformly.

4.3 A company clearly has the right to make and enforce reasonable rules to govern employee performance and conduct. It is entitled to a disciplined workforce. This means that employees can be expected to comply with rules that are reasonable and understood.

Progressive Discipline

4.4 Any disciplinary action may, ultimately be resolved in the courts where the burden of proof will be on management. Just Cause must be established for the action taken and the appropriateness of the penalty must be convincing.

5.0 JUST CAUSE FOR DISCIPLINE

5.1 A basic principle underlying most disciplinary procedures is that supervision must have "Just Cause" for imposing discipline. Even in the absence of a labor contract, "Just Cause" sums up the test used by most employees in judging whether management acted fairly in enforcing company rules.

5.2 The definition of **"JUST CAUSE"** varies from case to case, arbitrators generally have listed the following test for determining whether an employer had Just Cause for discipline an employee:

5.2.1 Was the employee adequately warned of the consequences of his/her conduct?

5.2.2 Did management (supervision) investigate thoroughly before administering the discipline?

5.2.3 The investigation must be completed before the decision to discipline is made. Such an investigation, where appropriate must include taking written statements from the employee(s) involved and from all others who may have witnessed the incident or who may have information to offer concerning the incident.

5.2.4 When immediate action is required, the best course is to **SUSPEND IMMEDIATELY, PENDING INVESTIGATION,** with the clear understanding that he/she/they will be restored without loss of pay if found not guilty. In such cases statements should be taken before the suspension takes place.

(Note: If more than one employee is involved in an incident, you must insure that ALL parties are suspended pending the outcome of the investigation).

5.2.5 Was the investigation fair and objective?

Progressive Discipline

5.2.6 Did the investigation produce substantial evidence of proof of guilt? It is not required that the evidence be conclusive or "beyond reasonable doubt", except where alleged misconduct is of such a criminal or serious nature as to damage the employee and seriously impair his/her chances for future employment.

5.2.7 Were the rules, order, and penalties applied even-handed and without discrimination? If enforcement has been lax in the past on a given rule or type of behavior, supervision may not suddenly reverse it and begin to crack down without having first warned employees, in writing of its intent.

5.2.8 Was the penalty reasonably related to the seriousness of the offense and employees past record? If the record of employee "A" is significantly better that that of employee "B", the company may properly give "A" a lighter punishment that "B" for the same offense, but the difference in their records must be very clear and well documented.

5.2.9 **Equal Treatment:** All employees must be judged by the same standards and the rules must apply equally to all.

5.2.10 **Rules of Reason:** Employees are protected against unjust discipline and permits a challenge to any company procedure that threatens to deprive employees of their rights.

5.2.11 **Internal Consistency:** The pattern of enforcement must be consistent, whether a company disciplines on a case-by-case basis, or uses a rule book.

5.2.12 **Personal Guilt:** Even though *two employees are involved in the same act of misconduct, the same penalty need not be applied* to each of them. Such things as **prior disciplinary records** may be considered. An employee being terminated must be suspended while "investigation" the latest violation; however, during this time final review of the documentation and/or approval of the discharge will take place **before** the discharge.

Progressive Discipline

6.0 SUMMARY OF DISCIPLINARY GUIDELINE

6.1 Key points concerning discipline.

6.1.1 Routine Problems: Follow a "stepped" process of discipline. The natural progression for ordinary, run-of-the mill problems should be as follows:

6.1.1.1 **Verbal Warning** (Documented on Counseling Statement)

6.1.1.2 Written Warning

6.1.1.3 **Suspension** (For two to four days)

6.1.1.4 Discharge

6.1.2 There is no magic. Sometimes, for example, there may be two suspensions and later, a discharge. Use common sense and, most importantly *****Document Your Actions***** including verbal warnings.

6.2 Serious Misconduct

In instances such as fighting, drinking on the job, falsification of company records and the like, it is appropriate to bypass the normal stepped process and suspend the employee(s) immediately pending investigation. In such cases, the employee should be told that, should the investigation clear him/her, he/she will be reinstated with full back pay.

7.0 SUPERVISORY GUIDELINES FOR DISCIPLINARY MEETINGS

7.1 The company has the right to prescribe reasonable rules of conduct in the workplace and to expect employees to abide by them.

7.2 Discipline should be viewed as corrective and not punitive or vindictive.

 **Progressive Discipline**

7.3 Keep detailed records. Many court cases have been won largely due to the precise and detailed records kept on discussions, disciplinary investigations and disciplinary decisions.

7.4 Clearly identify the rule infraction and present supporting facts.

7.5 The subordinate should be given the opportunity to present reasons, causes, and facts from his/her view point.

7.6 There should be a mutual effort to find a solution to the problem caused by the rule violation and a discussion of how repetition can be avoided in the future. A problem solving atmosphere is most likely to engage the cooperation of the employee and obtain a commitment to change the behavior in question.

7.7 The warning (or penalty) should be clearly spelled out on the counseling statement/

7.8 The employee should clearly understand what is expected of him/her in the future, together with the consequences of future offenses of the same nature.

Remember the importance of documentation. The counseling statement form has been designed to assist in the prompt recording of all the facts and the results of the disciplinary interview and provides evidence that the employee has seen and received a copy. It serves to verify the fact that discipline was clearly given for a specific rule violation --- and important point in the event that the issue is appealed to higher levels by the employee.

8.0 EMPLOYEE COUNSELING STATEMENT PROCEDURE

8.1 **This is the documentation;** it MUST be completed properly to back up your decision(s). The employee counseling statement is intended to document all significant contacts with subordinate employees. A proper completed counseling statement will serve as a valuable historical record and proof of fact, should an employee subsequently challenge an action by a supervisor.

Progressive Discipline

8.2 **The Procedure:** (Follow it –Follow it, to avoid a reversal in a hearing).

8.2.1 Indicate the type of counseling: Whether verbal or written warning, suspension or discharge in the space provided on the form.

8.2.2 Completeness: Insure that all appropriate sections of the form are completed in detail. Be specific. Leave no doubt as to the performance of the employee which led to the decision to issue a counseling statement. Do not hesitate to contact the President for assistance and guidance in completing this form.

8.2.3 Employee Comments: In all cases have the employee enter his/her comments on the form as indicated under item 6. Ask the employee to sign and date the form before giving him/her a copy.

8.2.4 Management Witness: When an employee is counseled, it is preferable to have a member of senior management present (this person should be a member of the same sex as the employee whenever possible). When an employee is counseled without a management witness present, and the employee refuses to sign the counseling statement, the counseling session should be reviewed immediately with the President present. A notation that the employee refused to sign the form should be made on the form, in the space provided for the employee's signature, and the President should initial and date the entry. The role of the President is just that, a witness, a quiet witness that does not make any comments while the counseling process is underway.

8.2.5 Disposition: Copies of the completed counseling statement are to be distributed, as appropriate, by the supervisor according to the distribution schedule indicated on the bottom of the form. ***Be sure to present a copy to the employee, even if they refused to sign and the President initialed the form.***

8.2.6 **Make sure that all spaces on the form which require that dates be entered are properly completed.** Many disciplinary actions have been set aside by the administrative law judge for either the lack of a date or an incorrect date, such as the year.

Progressive Discipline

ABC Company

Discipline Action Form

Date: _____

        FROM: Supervisor Name_____

        REGARDING: Employee Name_____

Check: __ **V**erbal Warning __ **W**ritten Warning __ **S**uspension __ **D**ischarge

1. I have made the following observation of the above named employee:

2. The Organization Policy or Work Rule which has been violated is:

3. The employee (has/has not) previously received disciplinary action for this policy infraction.

4. I have informed the employee that the matters set forth above are important because:

5. I have informed the employee of the following consequences if he/she fails to observe the standards set forth in Item 2 above:

These matters will be reviewed on an on-going basis

Following to be completed in all cases:

6. Employee's comments/remarks:

_____ _____ _____ _____
Employee Signature**   Date   Supervisor Signature   Date

**Signing this form does not indicate agreement, but only signifies that you have been informed of the action and you have received a copy of this counseling statement.

Review Action: Signed_____ Title_____ Date _____

___Original to Personnel File   _____Copy to Employee   _____Copy to Manager

Employee Compensation

1.0 INTRODUCTION

1.1. This Standard Procedure will outline the Employee Compensation policies and administration at the company.

1.2 Fair equitable pay for prompt, timely and accurate performance of assigned tasks and responsibilities is a major tenet of the employee/employer relationship. Each employee contributes to the success of the business.

1.3 The company will make every effort to see that the employees are paid at least equal to or better than those paid for similar work in this area.

1.4 The President is responsible for the administration of wages, salaries, commissions, and bonuses at the company.

1.5 This will be a general outline that will change as the company changes.

2.0 CONCEPT

2.1 Control of payroll costs is the responsibility of management. The President is responsible to administer the wage, salary and bonus program.

2.2 Positions in the organization are developed to fulfill a function for the business. All company functions have an economic value attached to the function.

2.3 The Functional Organization Chart is used to help determine the position's economic value, but this is the exception to the rule – not the "norm".

2.4 A position is only worth so much money to the company. It makes no difference who fills the position or how long.

2.5 Base pay is what the job is worth to the company; all other pay is based on a bonus or an incentive, based on budgetary performance.

2.6 Special cases may be found in the organization but all pay is still based on performance of some kind.

Employee Compensation

2.7   "Pre-planned" profits are determined by the OWNER.

2.8   Pay schedules are constantly reviewed and information logged for a periodic (one year) update of the schedule.

2.9   All employee pay rates are reviewed annually, as a minimum, with the employee during the budget preparation Information on all pay discussions is logged in the employee's personnel folder whenever a pay review is conducted.

3.0   PROCEDURE FOR DEVELOPING BASE RATES

3.1   The President will develop the base rate schedule for each position using the following systems:

3.1.1   On the Wage and Salary Survey Worksheet, identify each employee position within the company.

3.1.2   Title the worksheet with position and current wage.

3.1.3   Call the following organizations and companies for the current pay information at their site;

1) Local job service center
2) Local employment agencies
3) Local chamber of commerce
4) Local competition
5) Local college placement office
6) Local associations; and
7) National associations

3.1.4   Obtain the following: high dollar, low and average pay rate for the comparable company position and source of the information (Company's annual sales, Number of employees, Last pay adjustment, wage, and Benefit, and Bonus structure, et.al.)

3.1.5   Average the above information to create your anticipated wage range for each position.

 **Employee Compensation**

3.1.6   Update your information at every opportunity. Whenever someone calls you for salary information, someone quits for a better paying job or an interview is conducted and wage scale feedback is received.

4.0   EMPLOYEE WAGES

4.1   The employee wage structure will be determined annually by the President subsequent to an in-depth Wage Survey by the Administrative Manager in accordance with the Wage and Salary Survey program.

4.2   Supervisors will be responsible for the review and recommendation of the wage rate for all assigned personnel. The standing rates for new employees will depend on the levels of experience, education and ability of the particular employee.

4.3   Wages will be paid based on the satisfactory completion of assigned tasks and responsibilities.

4.4   The wage and salary rates for Fiscal Year 2000 have been reviewed and are published as an enclosure (Employee Wage Structure) and are currently in effect.

5.0   EMPLOYEE BENEFITS

5.1   The first ninety working days of full time employment are a probationary period. After the probationary period all regular full time employees are entitled to the company benefits.

5.2   The company is always attempting to provide for all the employees the best possible conditions and benefits and is always open to suggestions of employees for ways to improve existing benefits or possible new employee benefits, insurance plans, pension and morale programs.

5.3   Additions or other modification to the benefits are at the discretion of the President. Explanation, clarification, and administering of these employee benefits are the responsibility of each supervisor.

 **Employee Compensation**

6.0 BONUSES

6.1 Employee bonuses are paid to deserving employees as incentives for performance. A bonus may be paid to any employee at the President's discretion and is usually based on a recommendation by the employee's supervisor.

6.2 The company is currently developing a Profit Based Incentive Plan that will be based on exceeding a predetermined "bottom line" profit. When this plan is implemented, the company and employee's performance will be reviewed quarterly and the employee's share of the quarterly "bonus pool" will be distributed within three weeks of the close of the quarterly pay period.

6.3 Any employee that for any reason terminates their employment with the company prior to the close of the quarterly pay period shall forfeit all participation in the incentive program.

6.4 Substantial bonuses may be provided to certain designated employees who are directly responsible and accountable for the generation of company Profit and Loss.

7.0 SUMMARY

7.1 Asking other sources for information about their current wage and salary carries the responsibility to share your wage and salary information.

7.2 All of the company salary range rates will be updated once per year, as a minimum, prior to the start of the new fiscal year.

7.3 Wage Rates may go down as well as up. This depends on the local economy. By keeping the wage and salary rates current and the employees informed, there will be no surprises.

Employee Compensation
Wage and Salary Survey Worksheet

Position:	Current Wage:
Comments:	

Source:		Date:
Department:		# Employees:
Job Title:		
Minimum Pay:	Average Pay:	Top Pay:

Source		Date:
Department:		# Employees:
Job Title:		
Minimum Pay:	Average Pay:	Top Pay:

Profit Based Incentive Plan

INTRODUCTION

1.1   This procedure provides an outline for an incentive compensation plan for the company's eligible employees.

2.0   CONCEPT

2.1   Personnel performance and productivity are significant determining factors in the future growth of any company. Once fiscal goals are set, personnel must focus their efforts on meeting and exceeding the pre-planned profit goals of management.

2.2   Profit goals should be conservative, realistic, and attainable. When realized profits, however, exceed set goals, employees should be rewarded, since they contributed to that achievement.

3.0   FORMAT

3.1   Prior to the start of the fiscal year, the President selects those employees who will participate in the Profit Based Incentive Plan and assigns a specific number of shares to each participant.

3.2   The President declares a bonus to be put into a pool. The amount of funds to be distributed will be determined by profitability. Once a certain level of pre-tax profitability is reached, the company will share with plan participants the profits above this level. An amount up to a maximum of $xxxx per month will be added to the incentive pool for a grand total of $xxxx per quarter.

3.3   **IF PROFIT IS NOT REACHED, NO INCENTIVE COMPENSATION WILL BE PAID.**

3.4   We will announce the amount of money that is being added to the pool each month after the closing of the books for the month. (Usually the 5th day of the following month).

4.0   PROCEDURE

4.1   The following schedule illustrates who is eligible for the plan and the potential payoff if a profit is exceeded and the total pool contribution of $xxxx is met in any quarter.

Profit Based Incentive Plan

Potential payoff to participating personnel is determined by multiplying the total shares assigned to each person by **the par value per share.**

Position	Number of Shares	x	Par Value	x	Number Personnel	=	Potential Payoff
Tech Manager	19		180		2		6840
IT Manager	17		180		1		3060
Lab Technician	5		180		4		3600

4.1   In this example 25 shares remain unallocated. This allows for additional shares to be given to new people entering the Incentive Plan in the future as the company grows. Until this occurs the residual money in the pool could be retained in the pool, given out in a secondary distribution following the same structure as the first or given as special award to deserving employees at the President's discretion.

5.0   WHAT IS A SHARE AND WHO GETS ONE

5.1   The President sets the total number of shares.   In the Year XXXX, the total amount of shares will be 100.

5.2   Each position is allocated shares for each year. Using the Organization Chart, shares or fractions of shares, could be allocated by position, plus special consideration based on the individual's value to the company.

5.3   People may have extra shares for any number of reasons, i.e.: good work, new profit improvement ideas, outstanding behavior. Each employee's shares remain set for the fiscal year.

5.4   Shares may be reduced for problem employees.

5.5   How much an employee can receive of his/her share is determined by the overall rating achieved on his/her evaluation covering that period of time.

Profit Based Incentive Plan

5.5.1   If an employee's evaluation score is 95 – 100 % he/she will receive 100% of the funds available to him/her.

5.5.2   If an employee's evaluation score is 90 – 94.9% he/she will receive 85% of the funds available to him/her.

5.5.3   If the employee's evaluation score is 85-89.9% he/she will receive 75% of the funds available to him/her.

5.5.4   Of an employee's evaluation score is 80-84% he/she will receive 50% of the funds available to him/her.

5.5.5   **If the employee's evaluation score is below 80%, then he/she will not receive any of the payout from the program. (If the employee did not help earn the profit, then he/she should not be rewarded for just doing the job.)**

6.0   RULES OF THE PLAN

6.1   The President has the right to extend, modify or terminate the plan upon written notice to the participants.

6.2   The internal accounting records of the company will be control in all matters.

6.3   Each participating employee must receive an above average rating on his/her performance evaluation, or their respective payoff (or a portion of the pay off) will be retained by the company.

6.4   An employee who is hired after the start of the bonus period but who was chosen to participate in the plan will receive his/her pay on a pro rated basis (e.g.: each month equals 1/3 of the payoff).

6.5   If an employee leaves the company prior to the payoff for any reason other than retirement, his/her payoff will be retained by the company.

6.6   The company administrative manager will compute amount available for the plan on a quarterly basis and amount per share. Upon receiving this information, the President will inform all plan participants.

6.7   Payment will be made no later than three (3) weeks after closing the books for the quarter and the President has completed the review of company financial records.

Profit Based Incentive Plan

6.8 **This plan supersedes all other bonus and incentive plans.**

7.0 CONCLUSION

7.1 This plan is based upon the principle that the company must win first and the employees will win next.

7.2 The plan focuses employees' efforts on achieving company goals.

7.3 To be effective, the Plan must be explained and understood by all.

7.4 For best effect, a copy of the Plan and a list of its chosen participants will be given to each participant.

www.ingramcontent.com/pod-product-compliance
Lightning Source LLC
Chambersburg PA
CBHW050752180526
45159CB00003B/1439